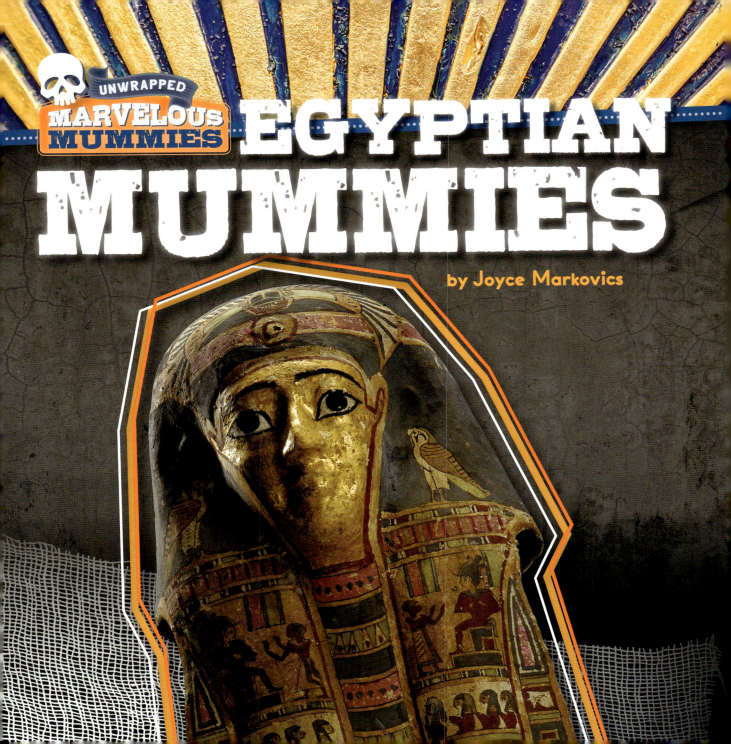

MARVELOUS MUMMIES
UNWRAPPED

EGYPTIAN MUMMIES

by Joyce Markovics

Published in the United States of America by Cherry Lake Publishing Group
Ann Arbor, Michigan
www.cherrylakepublishing.com

Reading Adviser: Marla Conn, MS Ed., Literacy specialist, Read-Ability, Inc.
Content Adviser: Owen Beattie, PhD
Book Designer: Ed Morgan

Photo Credits: © Smithsonian American Art Museum, Gift of John Gellatly, cover and title page; © Vladimir Wrangel/Shutterstock, TOC; © Wikimedia Commons, Jean-Pierre Dalbéra, 4; © Vladimir Wrangel/Shutterstock, 4–5; Wikimedia Commons, 5; © Roland Unger, 6; © LukeandKarla.Travel/Shutterstock, 7; © Barry Iverson/Alamy Stock Photo, 8; © Wikimedia Commons, 9; © Rik85/Shutterstock, 10; © Goran Bogicevic/Shutterstock, 11; © matrioshka/Shutterstock, 12–13; © Mikhail Zahranichny/Shutterstock, 14; © Wikimedia Commons, 15; © Jose Ignacio Soto/Shutterstock, 16–17; Wikimedia Commons, 17; © Anton_Ivanov/Shutterstock, 18–19; Wikimedia Commons, 19 top; © Danita Delimont/Alamy Stock Photo, 20; Wikimedia Commons, 21.

Copyright © 2021 by Cherry Lake Publishing Group
All rights reserved. No part of this book may be reproduced or utilized in any form or by any means without written permission from the publisher.

Cherry Lake Press is an imprint of Cherry Lake Publishing Group.

Library of Congress Cataloging-in-Publication Data
Names: Markovics, Joyce L., author.
Title: Egyptian mummies / by Joyce Markovics.
Description: Ann Arbor, Michigan : Cherry Lake Publishing, [2021] | Series: Unwrapped: marvelous mummies | Includes bibliographical references and index. | Audience: Ages 8 | Audience: Grades 2-3
Identifiers: LCCN 2020030232 (print) | LCCN 2020030233 (ebook) | ISBN 9781534180413 (hardcover) | ISBN 9781534182127 (paperback) | ISBN 9781534183131 (ebook) | ISBN 9781534181427 (pdf)
Subjects: LCSH: Mummies—Egypt—Juvenile literature. | Egypt—Antiquities—Juvenile literature.
Classification: LCC DT62.M7 M295 2021 (print) | LCC DT62.M7 (ebook) | DDC 962—dc23
LC record available at https://lccn.loc.gov/2020030232
LC ebook record available at https://lccn.loc.gov/2020030233

Printed in the United States of America
Corporate Graphics

CONTENTS

TUT'S TOMB   4

MAKING MUMMIES   10

MUMMIES FOR ALL   16

GOLDEN MUMMY CEMETERY   18

Mummy Map   22
Glossary   23
Find Out More   24
Index   24
About the Author   24

TUT'S TOMB

The year was 1922. **Archaeologist** Howard Carter was standing in a dark **tomb** in Egypt. His hands were shaking from excitement. "At first I could see nothing," Howard said. After his eyes adjusted to the light, he saw "gold—everywhere the glint of gold."

A gold object found inside the dark tomb

Howard had just discovered the tomb of **Pharaoh** Tutankhamen (toot-an-KAHM-uhn), or Tut. The king's mummy lay inside a solid gold **coffin**. It had been untouched for over 3,300 years!

Howard Carter looks at Tut's mummy. It was nested inside several other larger coffins.

King Tut was found in the Valley of the Kings. Many pharaohs were buried there. Tut's tomb, however, was the only one discovered that had not been robbed.

Howard and other scientists opened the gold coffin. Inside they found King Tut's mummy wrapped in strips of linen. On his head was a gold death mask. The scientists carefully removed the mask and unwrapped the body. Between the wrappings were gold charms believed to protect the body.

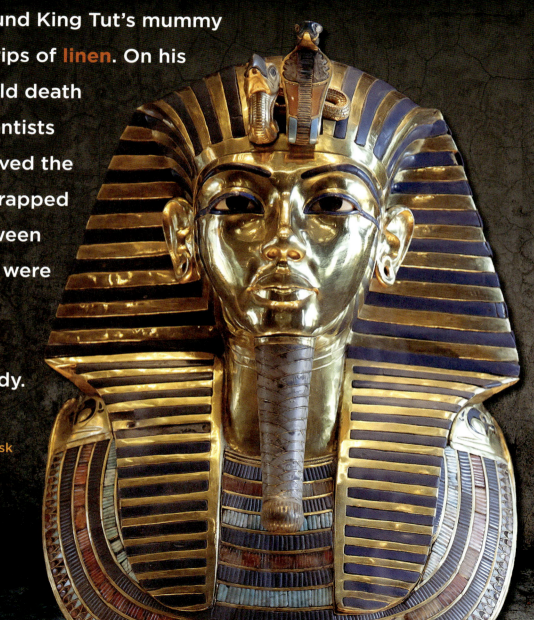

Tut's gold death mask

The scientists were amazed when they saw the mummy's face. Tut had high cheekbones, a small nose, and teeth that stuck out. The mummy's skin was cracked yet intact.

The pharaoh's face

A mummy is a dead person whose flesh and skin have been preserved in some way. King Tut's skin darkened in the coffin over time. He likely had brown skin when he was alive.

Over many years, scientists examined every inch of King Tut's body. They figured out that he was about 5 feet 6 inches (1.7 meters) tall. After looking at his bones, the scientists were also able to tell that Tut was about 19 when he died. And one of Tut's knees was broken just before he died.

Modern scientists looking at Tut's mummy

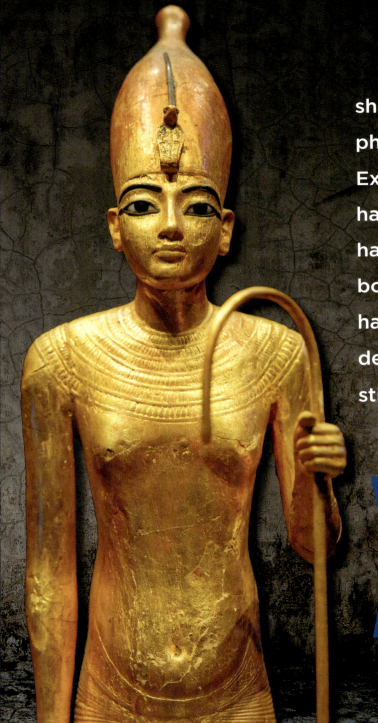

Later examinations showed that the young pharaoh had deformed feet. Experts think he might have had a bone disease. Tut also had malaria. Along with the bone disease, this might have led to the king's early death. However, experts are still studying the body.

Tut was buried with more than 100 canes, or walking sticks. Canes were often buried with pharaohs. But could they also tell us that Tut had trouble walking?

MAKING MUMMIES

The ancient Egyptians made tens of millions of mummies! They believed that when someone dies, the person's spirit, or soul, lives on in the afterlife. To get to the afterlife, however, the spirit needs a body.

For ancient Egyptians, death was a passage to another world.

mummies. That way, the bodies would be preserved for hundreds or thousands of years. Each mummy then is like a snapshot of the past.

Ancient Egyptians first started making mummies around 3000 BCE.

The word *embalmer* comes from balsam. Balsam is an oil from a plant that Egyptians used to make mummies.

Making a mummy in ancient Egypt took up to 70 days. First, the embalmer removed all the **organs** from the dead body except for the heart. Ancient Egyptians believed the heart was where thoughts and feelings came from.

Anubis is the Egyptian god of mummification. He's usually shown with the head of a jackal, a type of wild dog.

Then the mummy maker made a hole in the head or nose. A long, hooked tool, like an eggbeater, was inserted into the head. The tool was used to **liquefy** the brain. Then the brain was poured out of the head!

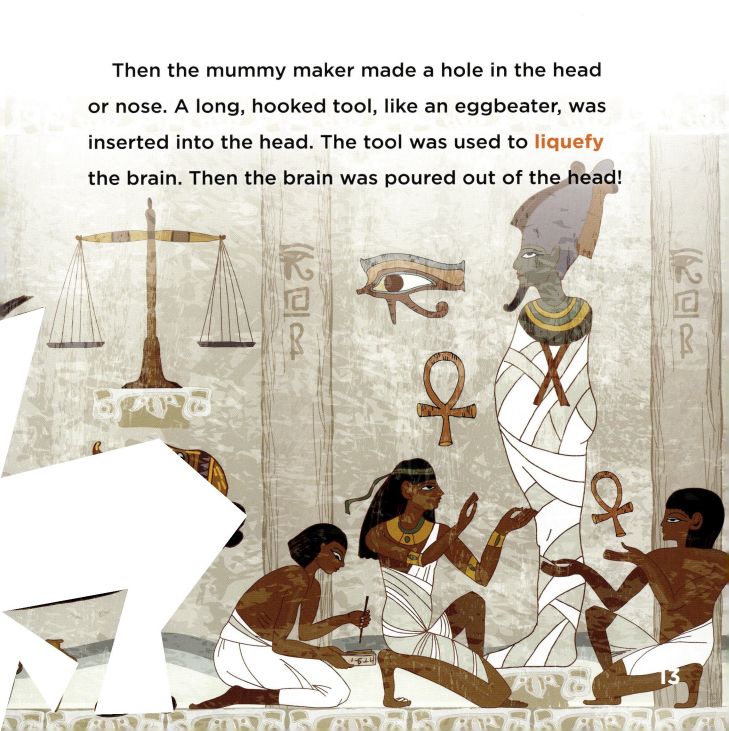

Next, the embalmer washed the body. It was dried using natron, a kind of salt. After several weeks, the body was coated in oils and resin. Finally, the mummy was wrapped in about 150 yards (137 m) of linen. That's enough to stretch the length of a football field almost two times!

After being dried, the inside of the mummy was packed with linen or other stuffing. This helped give the body a natural shape.

The mummy's organs were put in containers called canopic jars. The mummy and the jars were placed in a tomb. If the tomb belonged to a pharaoh, it was filled with treasures. For King Tut, these things included gold jewelry, paintings, and statues. There was also a chariot and a chair for Tut to use in the afterlife.

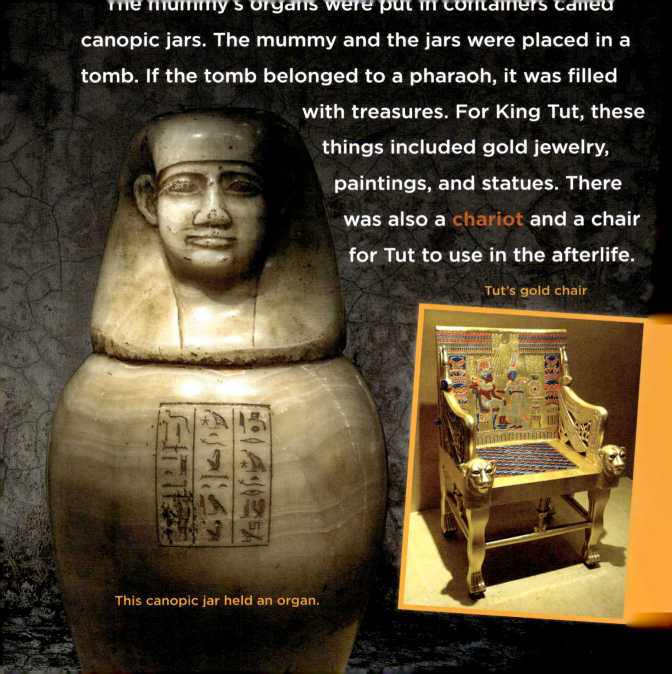

Tut's gold chair

This canopic jar held an organ.

MUMMIES
FOR ALL

At first, only pharaohs were mummified. Why? Mummification cost a lot of money in ancient Egypt. Before long, wealthy Egyptians began paying to have their dead bodies made into mummies. By 1550 BCE, anyone who could afford to was mummified.

It's thought that over 70 million mummies were made in Egypt during a 3,000-year period! Where did all the mummies go? Some mummies were buried together in large underground tombs. Over the years, many of these tombs have been discovered. Some were found by accident.

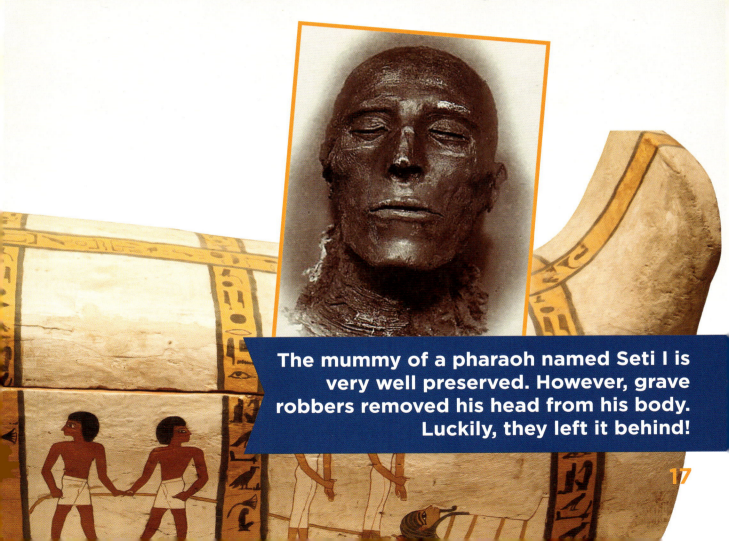

The mummy of a pharaoh named Seti I is very well preserved. However, grave robbers removed his head from his body. Luckily, they left it behind!

GOLDEN MUMMY CEMETERY

In 1996, a man was riding his donkey in the Egyptian desert. The donkey tripped in a hole. When the rider looked down at the hole, he saw a golden face looking up at him! It was an ancient masked mummy.

The man was riding near the Bahariya Oasis, an area in the desert where water is found.

The man told archaeologist Zahi Hawass about the golden face. When Zahi and his team began exploring the area, they found many more golden mummies. They had discovered a huge desert cemetery!

One of the golden mummy masks

Soon Zahi found over 100 mummies in a large tomb! They were stacked in **nooks** in the rocks. Many had beautiful gold masks. They were probably wealthy people, says Zahi. Others had no masks and were likely poorer people.

Researchers examining the nooks in the rocky tomb

Zahi thinks the cemetery might have belonged to several families. He believes there may be 10,000 more mummies in the area. But that will take years to confirm. The ancient secrets buried there will remain hidden for now.

By studying mummies, scientists uncover clues about the past.

MUMMY MAP

GLOSSARY

afterlife (AF-tur-life) the life a living thing has after dying

ancient (AYN-shuhnt) very old

archaeologist (ahr-kee-AH-luh-jist) someone who studies the past by digging up and examining old things

cemetery (SEM-ih-ter-ee) an area of land where dead bodies are buried

chariot (CHA-ree-uht) a small cart drawn by horses

coffin (KAWF-in) a box in which a dead person is buried

deformed (dih-FORMD) twisted, bent, or disfigured

intact (in-TAKT) not broken or damaged; complete

linen (LIN-uhn) cloth that's made from a certain kind of plant

liquefy (LIK-wuh-fye) to turn into liquid

malaria (muh-LAIR-ee-uh) a deadly disease that comes from the bite of a mosquito

nooks (NUKS) small, private areas or places

organs (OR-guhnz) body parts that do particular jobs

pharaoh (FAIR-oh) an ancient Egyptian ruler

preserved (prih-ZURVD) protected something so that it stays in its original state

resin (REZ-in) a thick, sticky liquid that comes from trees

tomb (TOOM) a grave, room, or building for holding a dead body

FIND OUT MORE

Books
Carney, Elizabeth. *Mummies*. Washington, D.C.: National Geographic, 2009.

Owen, Ruth. *How to Make an Egyptian Mummy*. New York: Ruby Tuesday Books, 2015.

Sloan, Christopher. *Mummies*. Washington, D.C.: National Geographic, 2010.

Websites
American Museum of Natural History—Mummies in Egypt
https://www.amnh.org/exhibitions/mummies/egypt

NOVA—Egypt's Astounding Mummies
https://www.pbs.org/wgbh/nova/ancient/egypt-mummies.html

Smithsonian—Egyptian Mummies
https://www.si.edu/spotlight/ancient-egypt/mummies

INDEX

archaeologists, 4, 19
afterlife, 10, 15
Bahariya Oasis, 18, 22
bones, 7–9
canopic jars, 15
Carter, Howard, 4–5
coffins, 5–6
death mask, 6
disease, 9
embalmer, 11–14
Golden Mummy Cemetery, 18–22
Hawass, Zahi, 19–21
linen, 6, 14
mummy-making process, 10–15
organs, 12–13, 15
Pharaoh Seti I, 17, 22
Pharaoh "Tut" Tutankhamen, 4–9, 15, 22
resin, 14
tomb, 4–5, 15, 20
Valley of the Kings, 4, 22

ABOUT THE AUTHOR

Joyce Markovics digs mummies—and all kinds of curious things. She also loves learning about animals and people from the past and telling their stories.